DRUMSET BEATS AND FILLS FOR TODAY'S PROGRESSIVE MUSIC

BY JIM RYAN

ISBN 978-1-4234-2482-6

HAL•LEONARD® CORPORATION
7777 W. BLUEMOUND RD. P.O. BOX 13819 MILWAUKEE, WI 53213

In Australia Contact:
Hal Leonard Australia Pty. Ltd.
4 Lentara Court
Cheltenham, Victoria, 3192 Australia
Email: ausadmin@halleonard.com.au

Visit Hal Leonard Online at
www.halleonard.com

ABOUT THIS BOOK

Since 1979, Jim Ryan has performed and recorded with numerous bands in various musical styles throughout the Midwest and South of the United States. He has published four drum instruction books as well as over 30 snare drum solos. Jim is currently teaching, recording, and performing in the St. Louis, Missouri area.

Visit **www.druminstructor.net** for more information on his other books *Rhythmic Movements* for snare drum; *Rhythmic Aerobics–Drumset Beats and Fills for Today's Musician*; *Rhythmic Aerobics Volume II–Drumming for Rhythms of Shuffle, Swing, Six-Eight and Odd Time Signatures*; and a collection of snare drum solos.

ACKNOWLEDGMENTS

I would like to express my thanks and appreciation to the following people for their assistance in the publication of this book: Thomas and Jean Ryan for buying my first drumset and for all their patience and support from the beginning; Bill Rathbun for teaching me to read music all those years ago; Austin Smith for providing the drums to record the CD; Tony Crowell for his illustration work; Terry Ryan for setting up the computer system; all my students for their inspiration; and God for making this project possible.

ABOUT THE CD

The first several beats of each chapter have been included on the CD, and are indicated with an audio track icon. Each beat is preceded by one measure of "clicks." On the CD tracks, beats that include a fill will repeat and play the first measure of the beat again. Other tracks simply play the beat four times, as notated.

CONTENTS

LEGEND

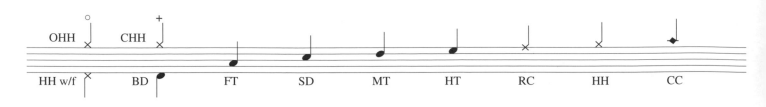

OHH = Open Hi-Hat

CHH = Closed Hi-Hat

HH w/f = Hi-Hat with foot

BD = Bass Drum

FT = Floor Tom

SD = Snare Drum

MT = Medium Tom

HT = High Tom

RC = Ride Cymbal

HH = Hi-Hat

CC = Crash Cymbal

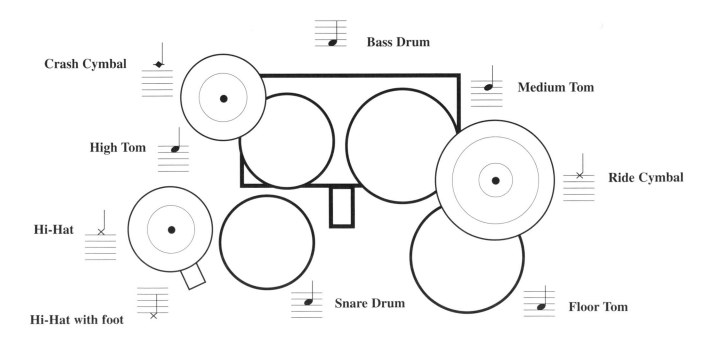

INTRODUCTION

Drumset Beats and Fills for Today's Progressive Music is an advanced instruction book for those wanting to develop skills for a wide variety of musical situations. I refer to the words "progressive music" in the title as being both advanced and modern with syncopation. You'll find an abundance of challenging material arranged in four-measure exercises contained herein.

This book focuses on nine areas of drumming: snare/bass thirty-second notes, sixteenth-note triplet beats, thirty-second notes with the hi-hat, funk shuffles, shuffle rhythms, swing rhythms, six-eight rhythms, fusion rhythms, and odd time signatures. It's not just a book to see how many notes one can play in a measure, rather a book that helps the player to maintain fluidity between the beat and fill. Include *Drumset Beats and Fills for Today's Progressive Music* as part of your practice sessions, and you'll increase your proficiency in timing, technique, and dexterity.

Drummers can benefit through books such as this that focus on a specific topic. It is advantageous to include material for your practice sessions that cover a variety of music styles. This book will help one become diversified with the challenges drummers encounter. There will be some pages that are very difficult to play, and so you should spend more time with those pages or sections.

Make sure a metronome is used when practicing, and try to repeat each exercise many times without stopping. Play the beats and fills until they feel easy to do, and make sure your timing doesn't fluctuate.

Try to experiment with your drumset. Substitute the ride cymbal for the hi-hat or even the cowbell. Play with four-way independence. The sticking included is for right-handed players. If you play left-handed, then reverse the sticking or use your own if it makes you feel more comfortable. Place accents in different areas of the measure and experiment with different dynamic levels. The beats and fills in this book will ideally be played on a five-piece drumset (see drumset layout on page 4), but of course can be customized to fit the size of your set. A crash appears occasionally on beat one of the first measure. It should be played only after you have finished the fill and are repeating the entire four-measure phrase. There are many ways to explore and learn from the written part of this text by developing your own substitutions. All that is required is a little independent thinking.

It is sincerely a pleasure to have you working with this book! I'm sure you'll find the beats and fills to be practical material for you in your pursuit to become a diversified drummer.

—Jim Ryan

1 Snare/Bass Thirty-Second Notes

On the CD tracks, beats that include a fill will repeat and play the first measure of the exercise again. In your practicing, repeat all exercises as many times as you wish.

♩ = 60–100

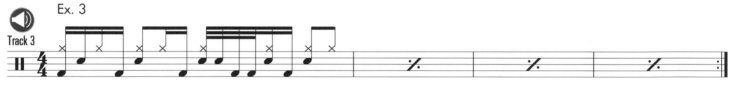

Ex. 7

Track 7

R L R L R L   R R L L R L R   L

Ex. 8

Track 8

Ex. 9

Track 9

Ex. 10

Track 10

R L R L L R   R R L L R   R R L L R L

(♦) = Play the crash symbol on beat one of the first measure on the repeat only, after the fill. Play the hi-hat all other times.

Ex. 11

Track 11

Ex. 12

Track 12

Ex. 13

Ex. 14

R L R   R R L L R   R R L L R   R L R

Ex. 15

Ex. 16

R L   R L   R L   R R L L R   R L

Ex. 17

Ex. 18

Ex. 19

Ex. 20

Ex. 21

Ex.22

Ex. 23

RL   LR   RRLLR   RRLLR   RRLL

Ex. 24

Ex. 25

Ex. 26

Ex. 27

RLRLR   RRLLR

Ex. 28

Ex. 29

Ex. 30

RRLLRLLRL   RL

Ex. 31

Ex. 32

Ex. 33

Ex. 34

Ex. 35

Ex. 36

Ex. 37

R L   R R L L R L R   R L R

Ex. 38

Ex. 39

R L R   R L   R L   R R L L R L R L R

Ex. 40

Ex. 41

Ex. 42

Ex. 43

Ex. 44

Ex. 45

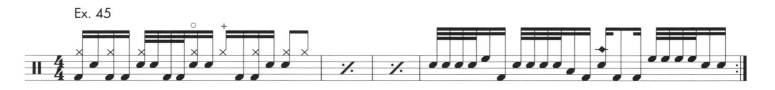

Ex. 46

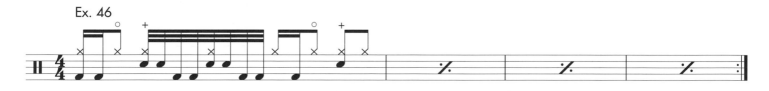

Ex. 47

Ex. 48

2 Sixteenth-Note Triplet Beats

♩ = 60–100

Ex. 49

Track 13

Ex. 50

Track 14

Ex. 51

Track 15

Ex. 52

Track 16

Ex. 53

Track 17

Ex. 54

Track 18

Ex. 55

Track 19

Ex. 56

Track 20

Track 21

Ex. 58

Track 22

Ex. 59

Track 23

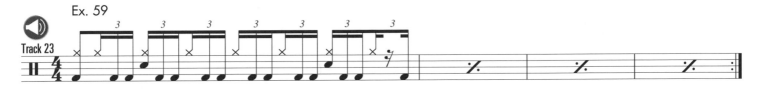

Ex. 60

Track 24

Ex. 61

Ex. 62

Ex. 63

Ex. 64

Ex. 65

Ex. 66

Ex. 67

Ex. 68

Ex. 69

Ex.70

Ex. 71

Ex. 72

Ex. 73

Ex. 74

Ex. 75

Ex. 76

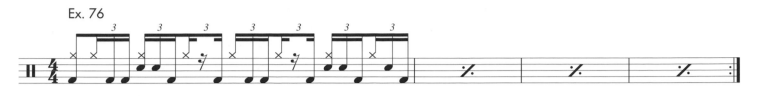

Ex. 77

Ex. 78

Ex. 79

Ex. 80

Ex. 81

Ex. 82

Ex. 83

Ex. 84

Ex. 85

R R L L R L R L R L

Ex. 86

Ex. 87

Ex. 88

Ex. 89

Ex. 90

R R L L R L R

Ex. 91

Ex. 92

Ex. 93

RRLLRLR

Ex. 94

Ex. 95

RRLLRLR   RLRL

Ex. 96

Ex. 97

Ex. 98

Ex. 99

RLRLRL   RRLLRL

Ex. 100

Ex. 101

RLRL   RRLLRL   RRLLRL

Ex. 102

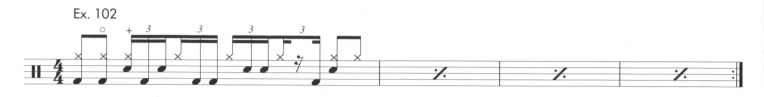

Ex. 103

Ex. 104

Ex. 105

RLRLRL R   RLRLRLRLRLR

Ex. 106

Ex. 107

RRLLRLLRRL

Ex. 108

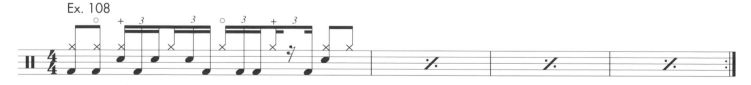

3 Thirty-Second Notes with the Hi-Hat

Ex. 117

Track 33

Ex. 118

Track 34

R L R L R L   R L R L R L

Ex. 119

Track 35

Ex. 120

Track 36

Ex. 121

R L R R L L

Ex. 122

R L R R L L

Ex. 123

Ex. 124

R R L L R L L R R L

Ex. 125

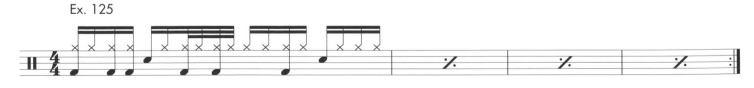

Ex. 126

Ex. 127

RLRLRL   RRLLRL   RRLLR

Ex. 128

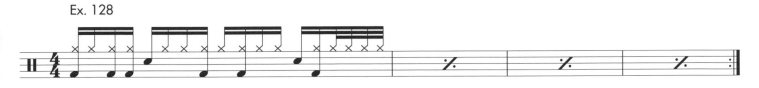

Ex. 129

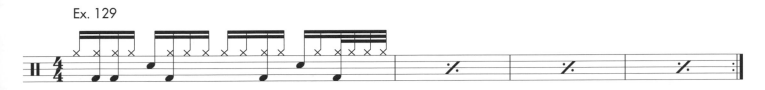

Ex.130

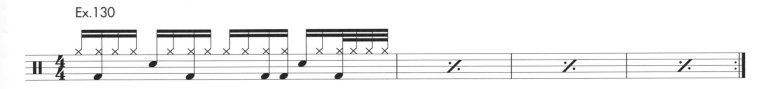

Ex. 131

RRLLRLRLRL   RL

Ex. 132

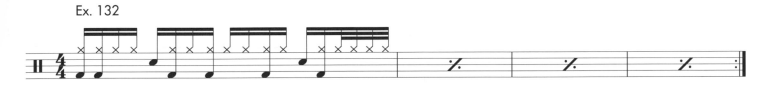

Ex. 133

RLLRRLL

Ex. 134

RLLRRLL

Ex. 135

Ex. 136

Ex. 137

R R L L R R L

Ex. 138

Ex. 139

R R L L R R L L

Ex. 140

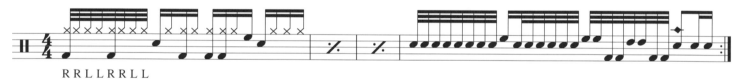

R R L L R R L L

Ex. 141

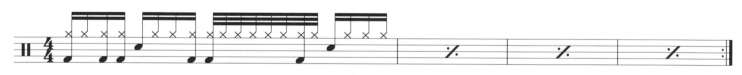

Ex. 142

Ex. 143

R L R R L L R R L L R L   R R L L R L   R R L L

22

Ex. 152

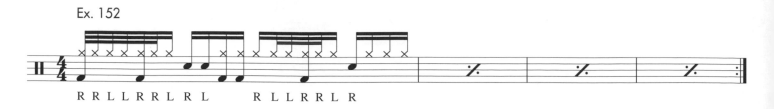

R R L L R R L R L   R L L R R L R

Ex. 153

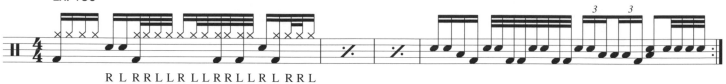

R L R R L L R L L R R L L R L R R L

Ex. 154

R R L L R L L R L R L L R L L R R L R

Ex. 155

Ex. 156

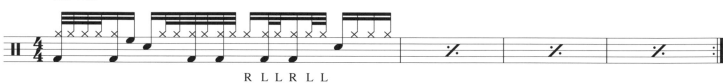

R L L R L L

Ex. 157

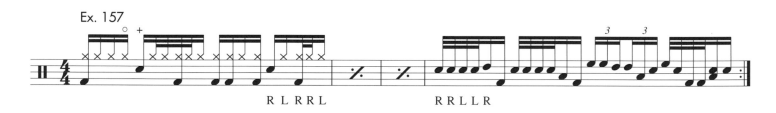

R L R R L   R R L L R

Ex. 158

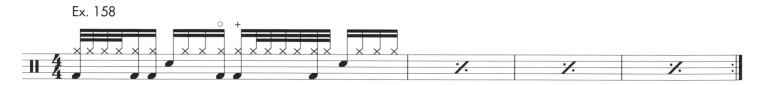

Ex. 159

Ex. 160

Ex. 161

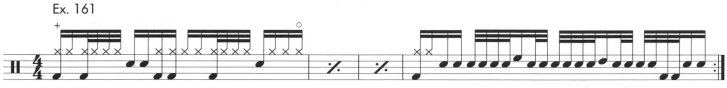

R R L L R L L

Ex. 162

R R L R L L

Ex. 163

R L L R L L

Ex. 164

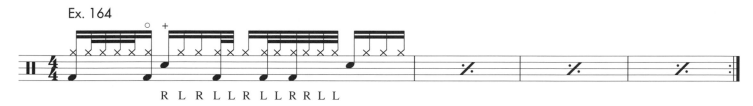

R L R L L R L L R R L L

Ex. 165

R R L L R L L

Ex. 166

R R L R L L

Ex. 167

Ex. 168

R L R   R   R L L R   R L L R R L L

4 Funk Shuffles

In addition to practicing with the hi-hat, as notated, also play the following beats with the ride cymbal. Alternate between the cymbal and bell as follows:

1) Play the bell only on the beat and the "and" of the beat (1 & 2 & 3 & 4 &). Play the other ride cymbal notes on the main body of the cymbal.

2) Create four-way independence by also playing the hi-hat with your foot on each beat or the "and" of each beat.

Track 37 plays Exercise 169 using the ride cymbal bell and hi-hat with foot as described above and as written. The remaining tracks in this chapter play each example as written.

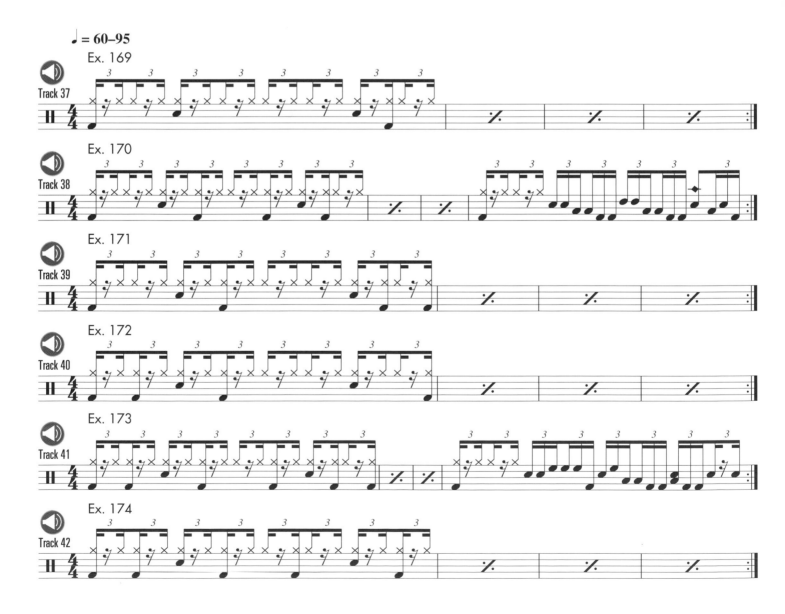

Ex. 175

Track 43

Ex. 176

Track 44

Ex. 177

Track 45

Ex. 178

Track 46

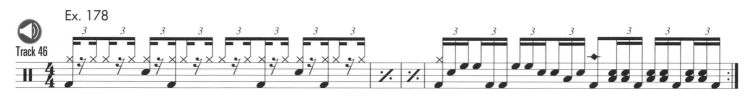

Ex. 179

Track 47

Ex. 180

Track 48

Ex. 181

Ex. 182

Ex. 183

Ex. 184

Ex. 185

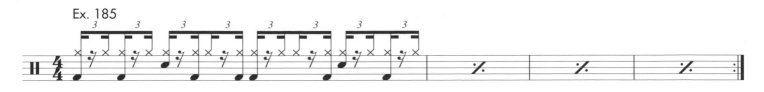

Ex. 186

Ex. 187

RRLLRLRL   RLRLRLR

Ex.188

Ex. 189

Ex. 190

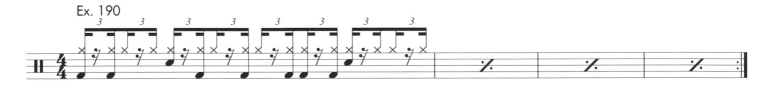

Ex. 191

RRLLRLR RL

Ex. 192

Ex. 193

RRLLRLR

Ex. 194

Ex. 195

Ex. 196

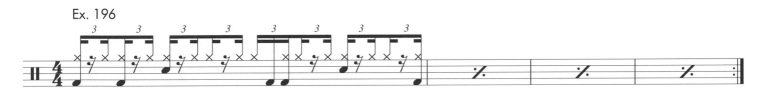

Ex. 197

Ex. 198

RRLLRLRL

Ex. 199

Ex. 200

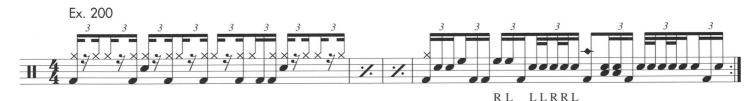

RL LLRRL

Ex. 201

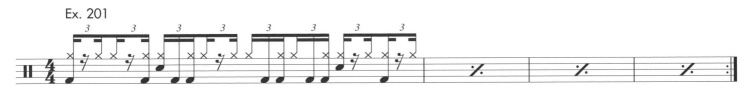

Ex. 202

Ex. 203

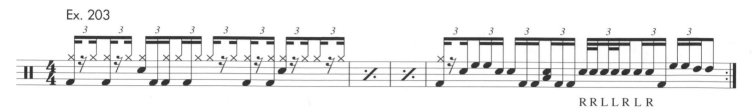

RRLLRLR

Ex. 204

Ex. 205

LLRRLL R LLRRLL

Ex. 206

Ex. 207

Ex. 208

Ex. 209

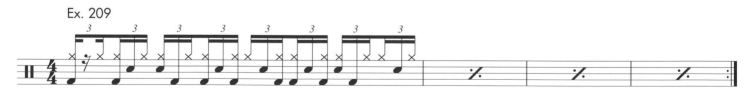

Ex. 210

RLRLRL   LLRRLLRLRL   LLRRLL

Ex. 211

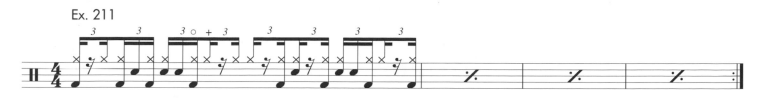

Ex. 212

LRRLLR   LRLRL   RL   LRL

Ex. 213

Ex. 214

RLR RL   RL   RL   RRL

Ex. 215

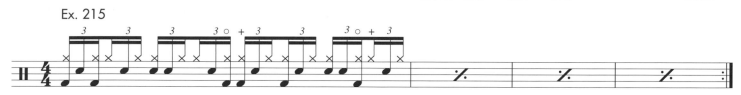

Ex. 216

LRLRRLRLLRLRRLRLRLRRLRLRLRRL

Ex. 217

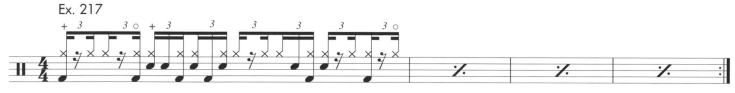

Ex. 218

RRLLRLLRRLR   RLRL   RRLLRRL L

Ex. 219

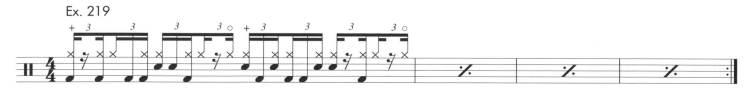

5 Shuffle Rhythms

Track 49 The exercises in this chapter may also be played using a complete eighth-note triplet or a quarter-note rhythm on the hi-hat. Track 49 demonstrates these two variations as applied to Example 220.

Ex. 227

Track 53
Part 2

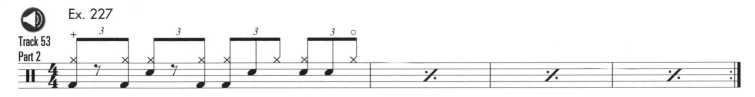

Ex. 228

Track 54
Part 1

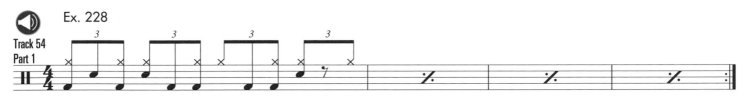

Ex. 229

Track 54
Part 2

L L R R L

Ex. 230

Track 55
Part 1

Ex. 231

Track 55
Part 2

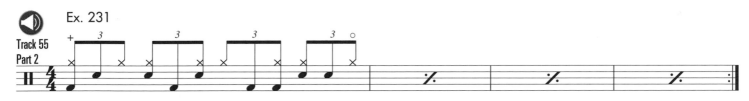

Ex. 232

Ex. 233

Ex. 234

Ex. 235

Ex. 236

Ex. 237

Ex. 238

Ex. 239

Ex.240

Ex. 241

Ex. 242

L   L R L   R L R L   R L

Ex. 243

Ex. 244

R R L L R R L   R R L L R

Ex. 265

Ex.. 266

R R L L R   L L R R L L

Ex. 267

Ex. 268

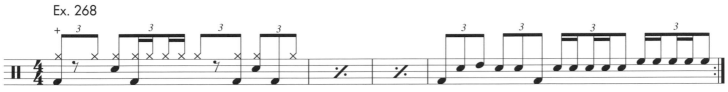

R R L L R L L R R L

Ex. 269

Ex. 270

R R R L L R   L

Ex. 271

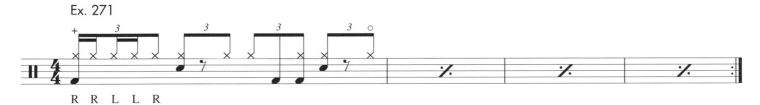

R R L L R

Ex. 272

R L R R L   R L R L

Ex. 273

6 Swing Rhythms

One-bar Exercises

In addition to the ride cymbal, practice the following swing rhythms with the hi-hat open on beats 1 and 3. Track 56 plays Exercise 274 with the hi-hat first, then as notated.

Ex. 280

R L R R L L R L R R L

Ex. 281

Ex. 282

Ex. 283

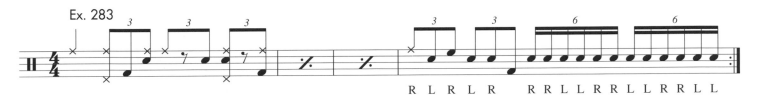

R L R L R   R R L L R R L L R R L L

Ex. 284

Ex. 285

Ex. 286

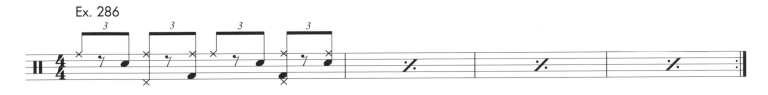

Ex. 287

R R L R L R R   R R L L R R L

At faster tempos, play the bass drum instead of the
floor tom on the above fill.

Ex. 288

Ex. 289

R L L R L R L L L R R L L

Ex. 290

Ex. 291

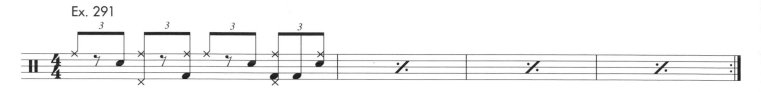

Ex. 292

L L R L L R L L R R L L R R L

Ex.293

Ex. 294

Ex. 295

Ex. 296

R L R L L R R L L R R L L R R L L

Ex. 297

Ex. 298

L L R L L   R R L L L R R L R L

Ex. 299

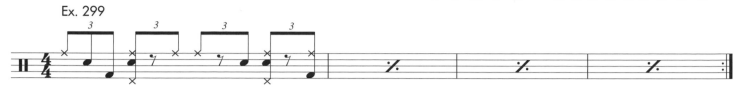

Ex. 300

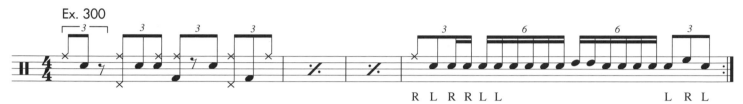

R L R R L L   L R L

Ex. 301

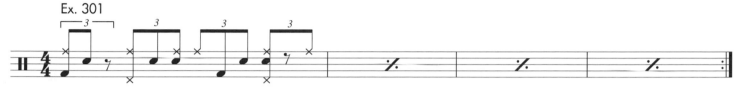

Ex. 302

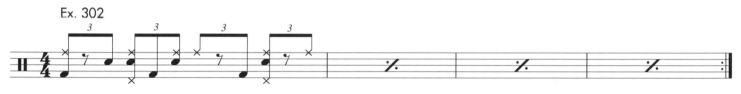

Ex. 303

L   L R   L L R R L L R R L R R L

Two-bar Exercises

♩ = 100–180

Track 59

Ex. 304

Track 60

Ex. 305

R L R L L L R L L L R R L L   R L L R R L L   R L L R R L L R R L L

Ex. 306

Track 61

Ex. 307

Track 62

R L R L L R L L R   L   R L L R R L R R L L R R L L R R L   L

Ex. 308

Ex. 309

R   L   R R L L R R L R R L L R L L R R   L   L R   L R   L

Ex. 310

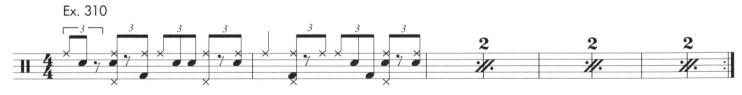

Ex. 311

L L R L L   L L R L L   R L L R R L R R L L R R L L R R L L R   L

Ex. 312

Ex. 313

L R R L R R L L R R R L L R L L R R L R L L R R L R L R L R R L L

Ex. 314

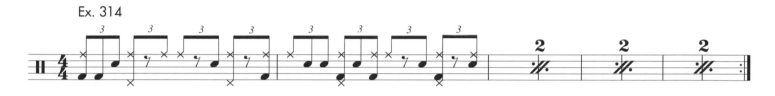

Ex. 315

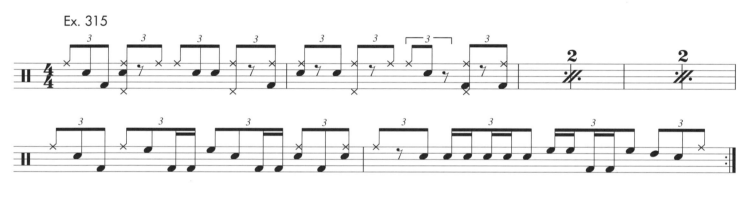

Ex. 316

♪ = Buzz stroke

Ex. 317

R R L L R R R R L L R L L R R L L

Ex. 318

Ex. 319

L L R L L   R L R R L R   L L R R L L R   R L L R R L L R R L R L

Ex. 320

Ex. 321

R   L R R L L R R L R R L L R L L R R L   R L L R R L L R R L   R L L R   L

Ex. 322

Ex. 323

L L R L R R L R L L R L R R L   R R L L R R L R L R   R L L R   L

$\frac{6}{8}$ **Rhythms**

Practice the exercises in this chapter as follows:

1) Play with the ride cymbal and play the hi-hat with your foot on (eighth-note) beats 1 and 4; 2, 4, and 6; or 1, 3, and 5.

2) Alternate between the ride cymbal and its bell. Play the bell on beats 1, 3, and 5; or 2, 4, and 6.

Track 63 plays Exercise 324 in three ways: the first two demonstrate numbers 1 and 2 above; the third plays the example as written. All tracks in this chapter start out with two measures of a dotted quarter-note count off. The exercises with fills repeat back to the beginning, playing the first two measures again.

Ex. 327
Track 66

R R L L R

Ex. 328
Track 67

Ex. 329
Track 68

R L L R R L R   R L   R L

Ex. 330
Track 69

Ex. 331
Track 70

R R L L R   R R L L R

Ex. 332

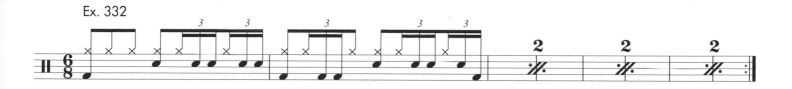

Ex. 333

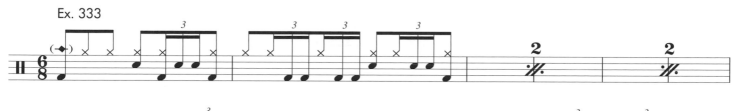

R R L L R L

Ex. 334

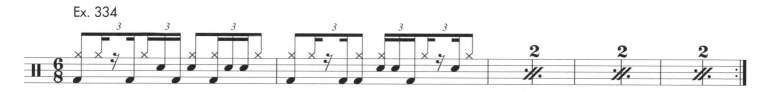

Ex. 335

Ex. 336

Ex. 337

R R L L R R L R R L L

Ex. 338

Ex. 339

R R L L R L R L R L L

Ex. 340

Ex. 341

R R L L R L L R L

Ex. 342

Ex. 343

R R L L R R   R R L L R R

Ex. 344

Ex. 345

R L L R R   R L   R R L L R R

Ex. 346

Ex. 347

R L L R R L L R R L L   R L L R R L L R R

Ex. 348

Ex. 349

R R L L R L R   R   R L   R L   R L

Ex. 350

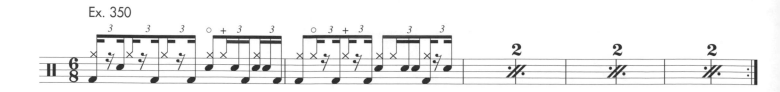

Ex. 351

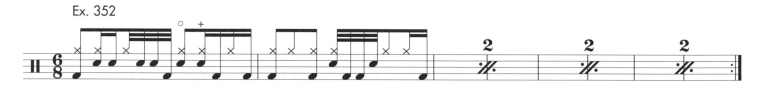

R L L R R L L R R L R R L R L L R L R L R L

Ex. 352

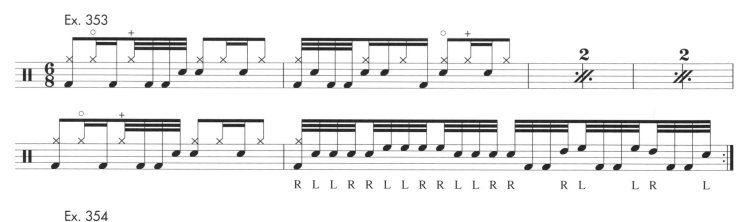

Ex. 353

R L L R R L L R R L L R R   R L   L R   L

Ex. 354

Ex. 355

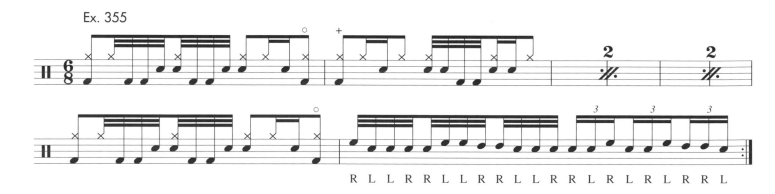

R L L R R L L R R L L R R L R L R L R R L

Ex. 356

L R R L R   R R L R L R L R R L R R

Ex. 357

R R L R   R R L L

Ex. 358

R R L R   R R L R L   L R R L L

Ex. 359

R R   R R   R R L R

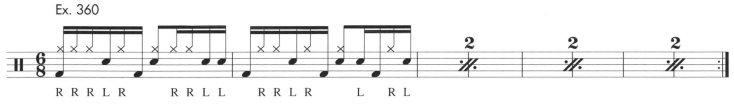

R L L R R   R L L R R L R L L R R L

Ex. 360

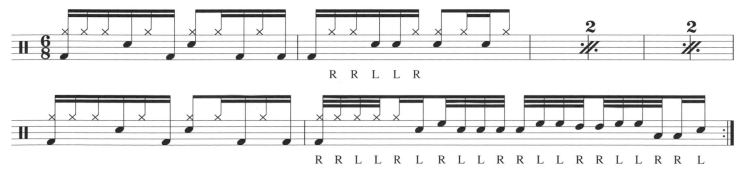

R R R L R   R R L L   R R L R   L   R L

Ex. 361

R R L L R

R R L L R L R L L R R L L R R L L R R L

Ex. 362

R R L R R   R L R R   R R L R R L

Ex. 363

R R L R R

R R L R R   R L L R R L L R R   R L   L R   R L

Ex. 364

R R R R L R R L R   R R R   R L L R R L

Ex. 365

L L R R L L R

R L L R L R R L L R L R L R

Ex. 366

R R L R   R R L L R L   R R L R R L

Ex. 367

L R R   R R   R R L R L   L L

L R R   R R   L L R R L L R R   R L R

Ex. 368

Ex. 369

R R L R R L   R R L L R L R R L

R L L R R L L R R   R L L R L R

Ex. 370

R L R R L R L L R L L

Ex. 371

R L L R R L L   L L

R L L R R L L   R L L   R L L R R L L R R L L R R   R L   L R

8 Fusion Rhythms

Ride Cymbal or Hi-Hat Rhythms

Play the following beats on the hi-hat first, as written, then on the ride cymbal.

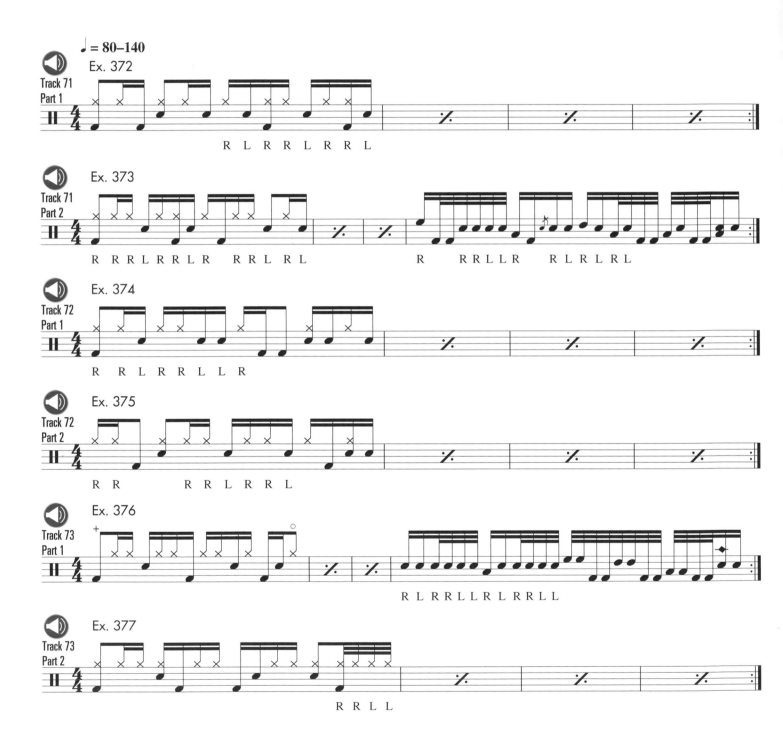

Ex. 387

R L R R L R R L L   R   R L L

Ex. 388

Ex. 389

Ex. 390

R L R R L R R   R R   R R

Ex. 391

Ex. 392

R L R R L L R R   R R L R

Ex. 393

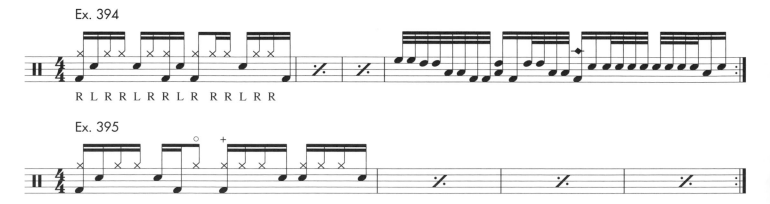

Ex. 394

R L R R L R R L R R R L R R

Ex. 395

56

Ex. 396

R L L R R L R L L R R L

Ex. 397

Ex. 398

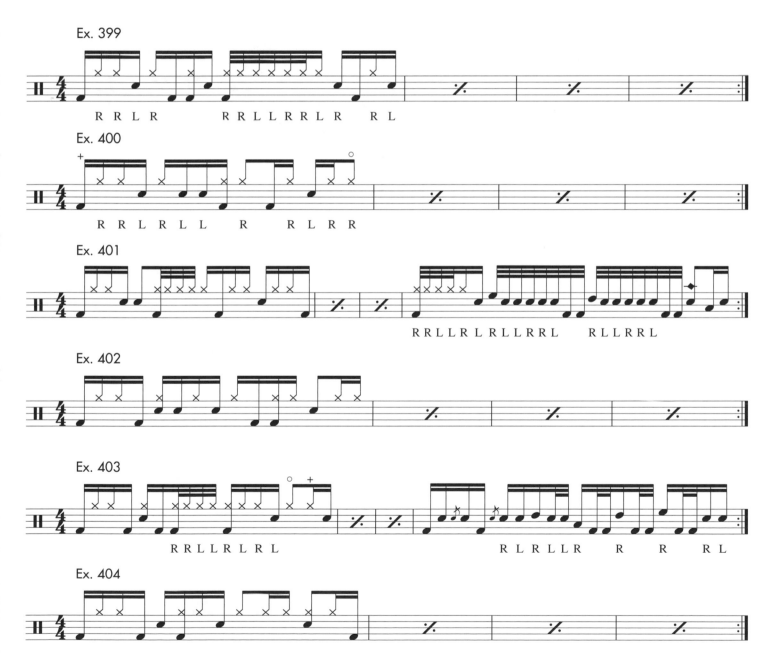

Ex. 399

R R L R   R R L L R R L R   R L

Ex. 400

R R L R L L   R   R L R R

Ex. 401

R R L L R L R L L R R L   R L L R R L

Ex. 402

Ex. 403

R R L L R L R L   R L R L L R   R   R   R L

Ex. 404

Ex. 405

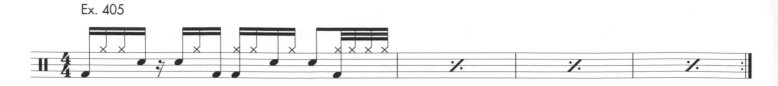

Ex. 406

R   RRLLRRLLRL

Ex. 407

R R L L R L L R L R

Ex. 408

R R L R L R R L L R   R R L L R L

Ex. 409

L L R R L L R R L

Ex. 410

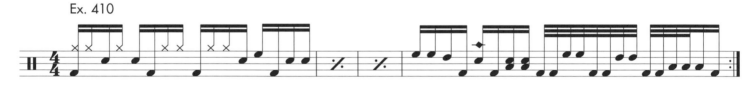

Ex. 411

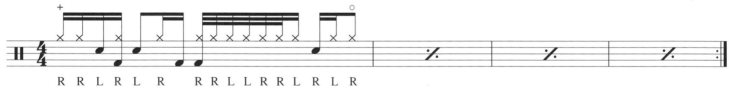

R R L R L R   R R L L R R L R L R

Ex. 412

R R L R R L R   R R R L R R R L

Ex. 413

R R L R L R   R L R R L R R L L   R   R L L R   R L L R   R L L

Substitute the cowbell for the ride cymbal in Exercises 426–449.

Ex. 432

R L R L R L L L L

Ex. 433

R L R R L L R L R L

Ex. 434

R L R L R L L L

Ex. 435

Ex. 436

R L R L L R R L L R L L R R L L R L L

Ex. 437

Ex. 438

R L R L R L L R L R L R L R R R L L

Ex. 439

Ex. 440

Ex. 441

R   L   R   L R L L   L   R L R L R   R L   L R   R L   L R   L

Ex. 442

Ex. 443

Ex. 444

Ex. 445

R L   L   L R   L R L   R R L L R R   R   R L   L R   R L R

Ex. 446

R   L R L L R   L R L R L

Ex. 447

R L L R R L R   R   R L   L R   L

Ex. 448

Ex. 449

Hi-Hat and Ride Cymbal Combinations

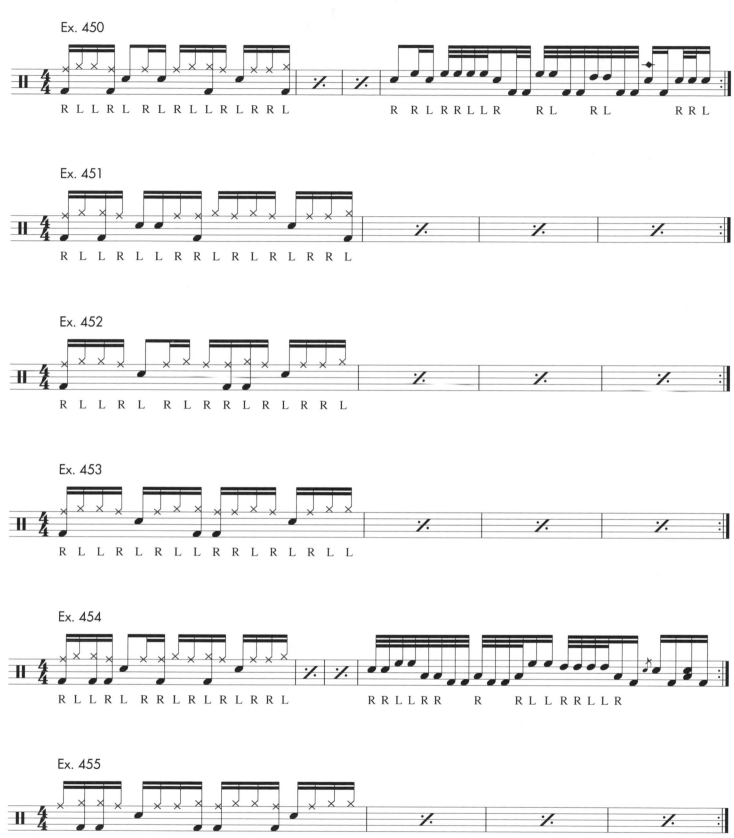

Ex. 450

R L L R L R L R L L R L R R L   R R L R R L L R   R L   R L   R R L

Ex. 451

R L L R L L R R L R L R L R R L

Ex. 452

R L L R L R L R R L R L R R L

Ex. 453

R L L R L R L L R R L R L R L L

Ex. 454

R L L R L R R L R L R L R R L   R R L L R R   R   R L L R R L L R

Ex. 455

R L L R L R R L R L L R L R L L

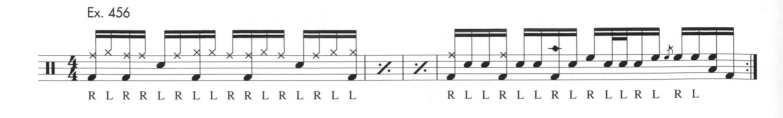

Ex. 456

R L R R L R L L R R L R L R L L   R L L R L L R L R L L R L R L

Ex. 457

R L R R L   R R L L R R L R L L

Ex. 458

R L R R L R L R L L R R L R L L   R L L R L L R R L L R R L

Ex. 459

R L R R L R L L R L L R L R R L

Ex. 460

R L R R L R R L R L R R L R L

Ex. 461

R L R R L R L R L L R L R R L   R L L R R L L R R   R L L R L L R R L R L L R R L

9 Odd Time Signatures

Rhythms in $\frac{5}{4}$

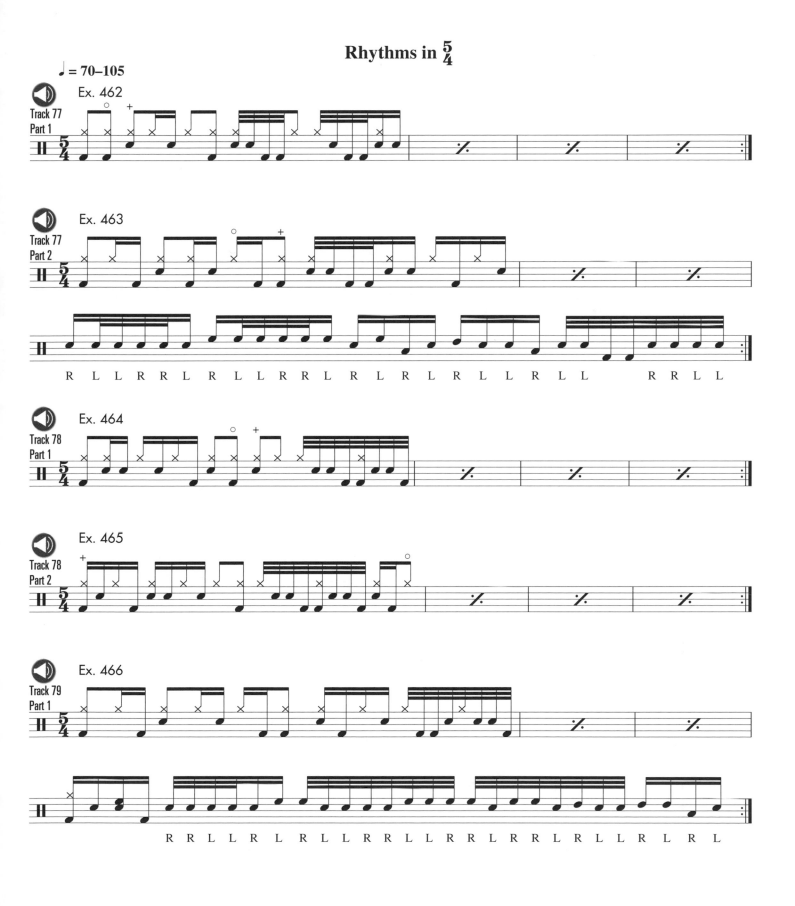

Ex. 467

Ex. 468

R L L R R L L R R L R   R L L R R L L R R L L R R L R L R L

Ex. 469

Ex. 470

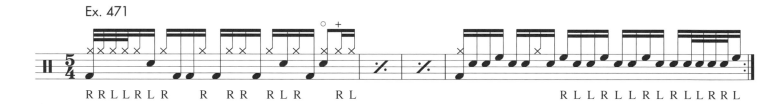

Ex. 471

R R L L R L R   R R R   R L R   R L   R L L R L L R L R L L R R L

Ex. 472

R R L R L L R L R L

Ex. 473

L L R R L L R L R R   R R L R R L R R L R

66

Rhythms in $\frac{6}{4}$

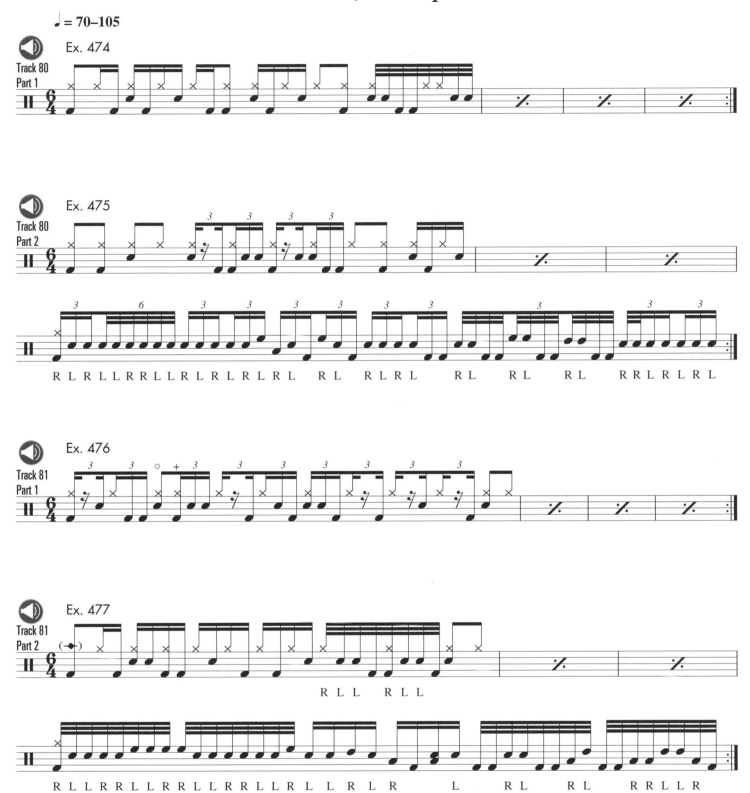

Ex. 478

Ex. 479

L L R R L R   L R   R L R   R L   R L R   R R L

Ex. 480

R L L R R L

Ex. 481

L L R R L

R L L R R L   L R   L R   R L L R L L

Rhythms in $\frac{7}{4}$

Ex. 487

R L L R R L L R

Ex. 488

R L R L L R R L L R L R L L R R L L R L L R R L L R R L R R L R L L R L R L R L   R L   R L   R L   R L

Ex. 489

Ex. 490

L R R L L R R R L R   R L L R R L R R R L R

Ex. 491

R L L R L R

Rhythms in $\frac{7}{8}$

♪ = 120–170

Ex. 492

Track 87

R L L

Ex. 493

Track 88

R L L R L R L L R L L R L L R L L R L R

Ex. 494

Track 89

Ex. 495

Track 90

Ex. 496

Track 91

R L R R L L R L L R L R L R L

Ex. 497

Track 92

Ex. 498

Ex. 499

R L L R R L   R L L R R L L R R L

Ex. 500

R L L R R L

Ex. 501

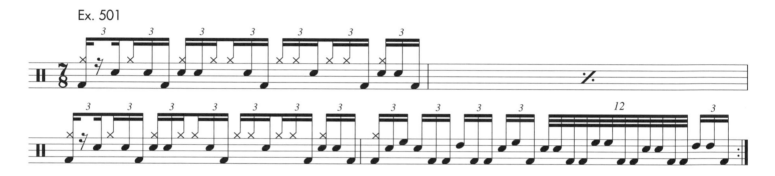

Ex. 502

R R L R R   R R L

Ex. 503

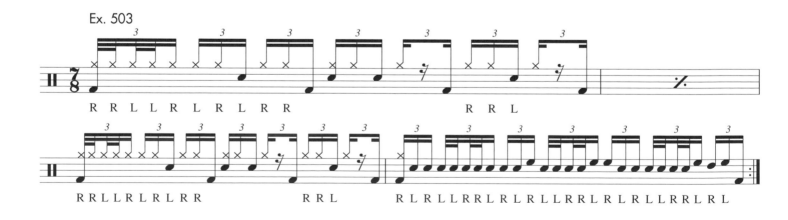

R R L L R L R L R R   R R L

R R L L R L R L R R   R R L   R L R L L R R L R L R L L R R L R L R L L R R L R L

Rhythms in $\frac{9}{8}$

All $\frac{9}{8}$ beats are in duple meter with an eighth-note subdivision of 2+2+2+3 (four beats per measure with the fourth being a longer beat).

Ex. 510

Ex. 511

RLLRLLRLLRLLRRLLR RLL

Ex. 512

RRLLRLRRLRRL

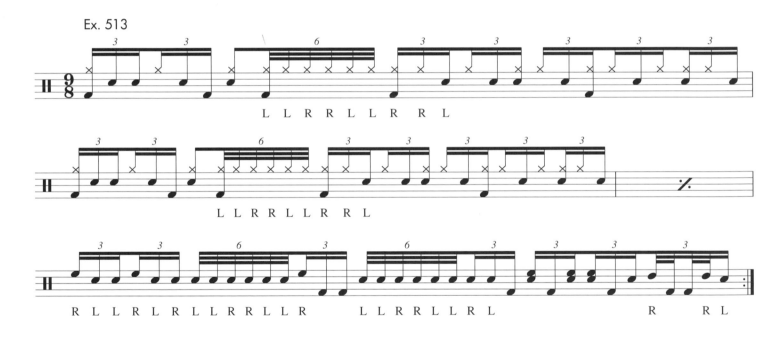

Ex. 513

LLRRLLLRRL

LLRRLLRRL

RLLRLRLLRRLLR LLRRLLRL R RL

Ex. 514

RLLRLRLLRRLRLRRLLRRLRLRRLRL

Ex. 515

RLLRLR LRRLRLRLRL RL RLRL

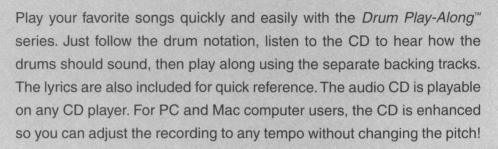

Play your favorite songs quickly and easily with the *Drum Play-Along™* series. Just follow the drum notation, listen to the CD to hear how the drums should sound, then play along using the separate backing tracks. The lyrics are also included for quick reference. The audio CD is playable on any CD player. For PC and Mac computer users, the CD is enhanced so you can adjust the recording to any tempo without changing the pitch!

Book/CD Packs

VOLUME 1 – POP/ROCK
Hurts So Good • Message in a Bottle • No Reply at All • Owner of a Lonely Heart • Peg • Rosanna • Separate Ways (Worlds Apart) • Swingtown.
00699742   Book/CD Pack $12.95

VOLUME 2 – CLASSIC ROCK
Barracuda • Come Together • Mississippi Queen • Radar Love • Space Truckin' • Walk This Way • White Room • Won't Get Fooled Again.
00699741   Book/CD Pack $12.95

VOLUME 3 – HARD ROCK
Bark at the Moon • Detroit Rock City • Living After Midnight • Panama • Rock You like a Hurricane • Run to the Hills • Smoke on the Water • War Pigs (Interpolating Luke's Wall).
00699743   Book/CD Pack $12.95

VOLUME 4 – MODERN ROCK
Chop Suey! • Duality • Here to Stay • Judith • Nice to Know You • Nookie • One Step Closer • Whatever.
00699744   Book/CD Pack $12.95

VOLUME 5 – FUNK
Cissy Strut • Cold Sweat, Part 1 • Fight the Power, Part 1 • Flashlight • Pick Up the Pieces • Shining Star • Soul Vaccination • Superstition.
00699745   Book/CD Pack $12.95

Prices, contents and availability subject to change without notice and may vary outside the US.

Transcribed SCORES®

Transcribed Scores are vocal and instrumental arrangements of music from some of the greatest groups in music. These excellent publications feature transcribed parts for lead vocals, lead guitar, rhythm, guitar, bass, drums, and all of the various instruments used in each specific recording session. All songs are arranged exactly the way the artists recorded them.

00672463	Aerosmith – Big Ones	$24.95
00672527	Audioslave	$24.95
00673228	The Beatles – Complete Scores (Boxed Set)	$79.95
00672378	The Beatles – Transcribed Scores	$24.95
00673208	Best of Blood, Sweat & Tears	$19.95
00690636	Best of Bluegrass	$24.95
00672367	Chicago – Volume 1	$24.95
00672368	Chicago – Volume 2	$24.95
00672452	Miles Davis – Birth of the Cool	$24.95
00672460	Miles Davis – Kind of Blue (Sketch Scores)	$19.95
00672490	Miles Davis – Kind of Blue (Hardcover)	$29.95
00672502	Deep Purple – Greatest Hits	$24.95
00672327	Gil Evans Collection	$24.95
00672508	Ben Folds – Rockin' the Suburbs	$19.95
00672427	Ben Folds Five – Selections from Naked Baby Photos	$19.95
00672458	Ben Folds Five – The Unauthorized Biography of Reinhold Messner	$19.95
00672428	Ben Folds Five – Whatever and Ever, Amen	$19.95
00672399	Foo Fighters	$24.95
00672517	Foo Fighters – One by One	$24.95
00672472	Goo Goo Dolls Collection	$24.95
00672540	Best of Good Charlotte	$24.95
00672396	The Don Grolnick Collection	$17.95
00672308	Jimi Hendrix – Are You Experienced?	$29.95
00672345	Jimi Hendrix – Axis Bold As Love	$29.95
00672313	Jimi Hendrix – Band of Gypsys	$29.95
00672397	Jimi Hendrix – Experience Hendrix	$29.95
00672500	Best of Incubus	$24.95
00672469	Billy Joel Collection	$24.95
00672415	Eric Johnson – Ah Via Musicom	$24.95
00672499	John Lennon – Greatest Hits	$24.95
00672465	John Lennon – Imagine	$24.95

00672478	The Best of Megadeth	$24.95
00672504	Gary Moore – Greatest Hits	$24.95
00690582	Nickel Creek – Nickel Creek	$19.95
00690586	Nickel Creek – This Side	$19.95
00672518	Nirvana	$24.95
00672424	Nirvana – Bleach	$24.95
00672403	Nirvana – In Utero	$24.95
00672404	Nirvana – Incesticide	$24.95
00672402	Nirvana – Nevermind	$24.95
00672405	Nirvana – Unplugged in New York	$24.95
00672466	The Offspring – Americana	$24.95
00672501	The Police – Greatest Hits	$24.95
00672538	The Best of Queen	$24.95
00672400	Red Hot Chili Peppers – Blood Sugar Sex Magik	$24.95
00672515	Red Hot Chili Peppers – By the Way	$24.95
00672456	Red Hot Chili Peppers – Californication	$24.95
00672536	Red Hot Chili Peppers – Greatest Hits	$24.95
00672422	Red Hot Chili Peppers – Mother's Milk	$24.95
00672551	Red Hot Chili Peppers – Stadium Arcadium	$49.95
00672408	Rolling Stones – Exile on Main Street	$24.95
00672360	Santana's Greatest Hits	$26.95
00672522	The Best of Slipknot	$24.95
00675170	The Best of Spyro Gyra	$18.95
00675200	The Best of Steely Dan	$19.95
00672468	Sting – Fields of Gold	$24.95
00674655	Sting – Nothing Like the Sun	$19.95
00673230	Sting – Ten Summoner's Tales	$19.95
00672521	Best of SUM 41	$29.95
00675520	Best of Weather Report	$18.95

Prices and availability subject to change

0308

Modern Drummer Books

From the publishers of *Modern Drummer Magazine*

Bill Bruford – When In Doubt, Roll

Designed for the intermediate-level drummer, this book is a collection of 18 of Bruford's greatest performances, with suggested exercises and insights from his years as one of the world's foremost drummers. Bill Bruford is best known for his work with Yes, Genesis, King Crimson, Al DiMeola, and others.
06630298 ....$13.95

The Best Of Concepts

by Roy Burns

Modern Drummer presents this compilation of articles in Roy Burns' popular "Concepts" series, which ran in the magazine between 1980 and 1992. Roy is a respected clinician and drummer who has worked with big bands, jazz acts, and on T.V.. This book features nearly 70 of his most enlightening writings and will be of great interest to drummers of all levels.
06621766 ....$9.95

The Best Of Modern Drummer: Rock

This special book is a compilation of the 50 best "Rock Perspectives" articles that have appeared in *Modern Drummer* magazine since its beginnings. The informational articles are packed with tips and instructions, and the authors include famous drummers like Neil Peart, Will Kennedy, Kenny Aronoff, and more. Includes lots of musical examples.
06621759 ....$9.95

The Best Of Modern Drummer
Volume 2

This is a collection of articles from 12 of *Modern Drummer*'s most popular columns, each dealing with a different aspect of the art of drumming. Includes a good balance of authors, with some articles written by name drummers, and some by the average drummer/writer with something of value to say to fellow drummers. Here is a book that makes valuable information readily accessible for anyone who may have missed it the first time around in *Modern Drummer*.
06630196 ....$7.95

Joe Morello – Master Studies

This is "the" book on hand development and drumstick control. *Master Studies* focuses on these important aspects: accent studies, buzz-roll exercises, single and double-stroke patterns, control studies, flam patterns, dynamic development, endurance studies, and much more!
06631474...$9.95

Drum Wisdom

by Bob Moses

Here is a drum book that offers much more than page after page of dull exercises. *Drum Wisdom* is a clear presentation of the unique and refreshing concepts developed by Bob Moses, one of the most exceptional drummers of our time. Topics include thinking musically, internal hearing, playing off of melodies and vamps, the 8/8 concept, understanding resolution points, drumming and movement, the non-independent style, and more.
06630510...$7.95

Carl Palmer – Applied Rhythms

Carl Palmer, one of the foremost drummers in the world, is probably best known for his work with Emerson, Lake & Palmer and Asia. His book contains rhythm exercises that can be used to develop the techniques that modern drummers need in a variety of situations. Contains transcriptions of 10 songs, including "Heat of the Moment" and "Brain Salad Surgery."
06630365...$8.95

The Great Jazz Drummers

by Ronald Spagnardi

The Great Jazz Drummers is an excellent reference for any drummer or jazz enthusiast. It features biographies and photos of 62 influential drummers, as well as a soundsheet featuring 16 artists demonstrating the gradual progression of jazz drumming through seven decades.
06621755...$19.95

New Breed

by Gary Chester

Gary Chester was one of the busiest studio drummers of the 60's and 70's and played on hundreds of hit records. His systems have been used and endorsed by drummers such as Kenny Aronoff, Danny Gottlieb, and Dave Weckl. This is not just another drum book, but rather a system that will help you develop the skills needed to master today's studio requirements. By working with this book, you'll improve your reading, concentration, coordination, right and left-hand lead, and awareness of the click.
06631619 ....$9.95

FOR MORE INFORMATION, SEE YOUR LOCAL MUSIC DEALER,
OR WRITE TO:

HAL•LEONARD®
CORPORATION

777 W. BLUEMOUND RD. P.O. BOX 13819 MILWAUKEE, WI 53213